POEMS FOR LOVE

More poetry available from
Macmillan Collector's Library

POEMS FOR LOVE

With an introduction by
JOANNA TROLLOPE

Edited by
GABY MORGAN

MACMILLAN COLLECTOR'S LIBRARY

This collection first published 2018 by Macmillan Collector's Library

This edition published 2024 by Macmillan Collector's Library
an imprint of Pan Macmillan
The Smithson, 6 Briset Street, London EC1M 5NR
EU representative: Macmillan Publishers Ireland Ltd,
1st Floor, The Liffey Trust Centre, 117–126 Sheriff Street Upper,
Dublin 1, DO1 YC43
Associated companies throughout the world
www.panmacmillan.com

ISBN 978-1-0350-2672-2

Introduction copyright © Joanna Trollope 2018
Selection and arrangement copyright © Macmillan Publishers International Ltd. 2018

1 3 5 7 9 8 6 4 2

A CIP catalogue record for this book is available from the British Library.

Cover and endpaper design: Daisy Bates, Pan Macmillan Art Department
Printed and bound in China by Imago

Visit **www.panmacmillan.com** to read more
about all our books and to buy them.

Contents

IF ALL THE WORLD AND LOVE
WERE YOUNG

DELIGHT IN DISORDER

LET ME NOT TO THE MARRIAGE
OF TRUE MINDS

MY LIFE CLOSED TWICE BEFORE
ITS CLOSE

Introduction

JOANNA TROLLOPE

I once had an Emma Bridgewater mug whose inscription read, 'True Love and High Adventure'. The inscription wasn't wrong. There is probably no emotional adventure in life like falling in love, nothing in our human experience that equals the sheer exhilaration of it. Other great happenings in life – marriage, childbirth, career and academic success – may well tap into other and more profound layers of the psyche, but for utter, heady, exultant jubilation, falling in love is it.

This anthology of love poems is proof – if we ever needed it – that down the centuries, the experience of falling in love has never, in its essence, changed. Social and cultural codes of conduct may have altered since anonymous poets wrote, or recited, the first versions of 'Scarborough Fair' or 'Blest, Blest and Happy He', but the emotion, the sensation that the true meaning of life now resides solely in a single person, hasn't. The rapturous surrender to feeling described by Robert Herrick, in 'The Shoe-Tying',

> Anthea bade me tie her shoe;
> I did; and kissed the Instep too:
> And would have kissed unto her knee,
> Had not her Blush rebuked me.

is eternal in its intensity. The only difference, under today's liberal flag, is that Herrick is unlikely to have stopped his kissing to spare Anthea's maidenly blushes. Apart from that, her instinctively provocative teasing, followed by her confused retreat, is timeless. So is the idea that women's clothing, especially if slightly dishevelled, is both a turn-on and a come-on. That young men of the fifteenth and sixteenth centuries were as inflamed by any 'sweet disorder in the dress' as any modern boy needs no searching out. The poetry of Shakespeare, Thomas Campion, Andrew Marvell, Ben Jonson and John Donne – all in this anthology – provides evidence enough. And in the great scheme of poetic expression of human emotion and sensation, they were quite late. Here is the Roman poet, Catullus, writing in the first century BC:

> My woman says she wants no other lover
>   than me, not even Jupiter himself.
> She says so. What a woman says to an eager
>   sweetheart
>   write on the wind, write on the rushing
>   waves.

No problem, then, to find evidence in the last two thousand years of what D. H. Lawrence called 'The wild chaos of love'. But ways of expressing it – the fashions of poetic language, if you like – have changed down the decades and centuries, and are very different. Or can be. No poet these days, for example, would write in the manner of Sir Philip Sidney in his famous 'The Bargain' – incidentally, Jackie Onassis' favourite poem – or even in the high-flown Victorian style of Elizabeth Barrett Browning's 'How do I love thee?'. The 'thees' and 'thous' of the past, the vogues for the pastoral (Christopher Marlowe) or the mythological (W. B. Yeats) were entirely of the poetic moment in their day, and part of their charm for the reader in the twenty-first century lies in their invocations of times past, with all the security of romantic hindsight. Even if modern reticence might flinch at composing with the emotional extravagance of Alfred, Lord Tennyson's 'Marriage Morning', it remains a very popular contemporary choice for weddings:

> Heart, are you great enough
>   For a love that never tires?
> O heart, are you great enough for love?
>   I have heard of thorns and briers.
> Over the thorns and briers,
>   Over the meadow and stiles,
> Over the world to the end of it
>   Flash for a million miles.

This poem, of course, references nature in a most evocative way. Using images of nature as a means of expressing being in love never goes out of fashion, nor does water – especially the sea – or flowers, or weather, or sunrises and settings, nor the ineffable ecstasy of solitude. Whatever changes there may be in the way emotion is expressed, the inner exultation remains a constant and finds an instinctive metaphorical ally in the natural world, be it a wild storm or a serene dawning, an ocean or a rose. It is as if people in love have always found themselves at their most primitively natural, taken prisoner by a feeling that insists upon complete surrender and the permission to say, with luxurious abandonment to an irresistible happening, 'I had no choice.'

Yet for all this community of rapturous feeling down the years, there is also a wish, as time passes, to take things to a more settled place, often expressed in poetic voices that cannot be dated to the literary fashions that prevailed in Tudor England or Victorian America or eighteenth-century Scotland. Often, and perhaps un-surprisingly, those voices are anonymous. Here are the opening lines of one such poem:

> Now you will feel no rain,
> for each of you will be a shelter to the other.
>
> Now you will feel no cold,
> for each of you will be warmth to the other.

And it ends,

> Go now to your dwelling place,
> to enter into the days of your togetherness.
>
> And may your days be good
> and long upon the earth.

This poem is known as the 'Apache wedding song'. It probably isn't very old, and it may well be Cherokee rather than Apache, but neither of those details matters, because it expresses what humanity longs for, the security of a safe harbour for one's emotional ship. It says what we need it to say, it promises that after 'the wild chaos' of falling in love, there will be a strong, trustworthy peace on which to build for the future. So, if it came from a recent romantic folklorist, rather than from an ancient tribal ceremony, it makes no difference, in essence. The feeling comes straight from the human heart, just as Shakespeare's sonnets do, or the quiet agony of Charlotte Mew's 'I so liked spring'.

Which brings me on to another aspect entirely, of falling in love. Which is the anguish. Bereavement, or the unrequited hankering for someone indifferent or out of reach, makes for powerful poetry. The human heart is a muscle as well as an organ, and it needs exercise, so when the natural outlet for its energy is cut

ff by death or deprivation, it faces a bleak prospect of
rustrated longing. Poetry, with its capacity for inten-
ity, can be the perfect outlet for feelings of emotional
despair. Here is Lady Catherine Dyer, on the miseries
f being without her late William, in 1641:

> My dearest dust, could not thy hasty day
> Afford thy drowsy patience leave to stay
> One hour longer: so that we might either
> Sit up, or gone to bed together?

here is actually, she thinks, no point in going on with-
ut him:

> Mine eyes wax heavy and the day grows old,
> The dew falls thick, my blood grows cold.
> Draw, draw the closed curtains: and make room:
> My dear, my dearest dust; I come, I come.

At least, one could think, she had had William – she
ad known the joy and attendant security of true and
equited love. But what about all those lovers doomed
) disappointment, to the acute unhappiness of not
aving their love returned? Few have the almost jaunty
an't-be-helped attitude of Michael Drayton's Eliza-
ethan sonnet, 'Since there's no help, come let us kiss
nd part'; much more common is the expression of the
retched pain of rejection, or of the realization that too
te really means too late. John Clare made no bones
bout his reaction to being told that he was not the man
r the girl he had set his heart on, and still obsessed
bout the very spot where she had told him that they
ere finished:

> 'Twas here she said farewell and no one yet
> Has so sweet spoken – How can I forget?

Even Wordsworth, not perhaps as known for delicate emotional suffering as for causing it, felt the sharp stab of emotional regret:

> She lived unknown, and few could know
>> When Lucy ceased to be;
> But she is in her grave, and, oh,
>> The difference to me!

But to my mind, nobody comes close to Emily Dickinson for sheer, frank confrontation of emotional loss. This poem of hers is mysterious as well as an expression of dreadful emotional wretchedness; we don't know if she was bereaved, or in love and rejected, or abandoned, or simply without somebody crucial to her happiness, like a family member. It was published ten years after her death in 1886. I'm going to quote it in full because it says so much in so few lines:

> My life closed twice before its close –
> It yet remains to see
> If Immortality unveil
> A third event to me
>
> So huge, so hopeless to conceive
> As these that twice befell.
> Parting is all we know of heaven,
> And all we need of hell.

So much for bitter heartache. But love poetry manages something else, something that does not swing wildly between the diametrically opposite poles of falling in love and having to somehow live without the object of one's love. And it is something that I might call universality, or completeness. Love is, in essence, the great leveller. It doesn't matter where you are born on the social scale, it doesn't matter about your level

f wealth, or literacy, or social prominence or worldly
nfluence. Love happens to everyone, however their
ndividual personalities choose to react to it, and this
quality is reflected, down the ages, by the poetry, from
pre-medieval aural ballads to modern pop lyrics. It also
doesn't matter how clichéd any aspect of romantic love
is in itself, because the first time it happens to you is
the first time in the history of the universe.

This aspect of love poetry is wonderfully bonding. It
links people together in a mutual understanding that
almost no other poetic genre can. We have, after all,
all been there, one way or another. Take first a rather
cheerful example – the familiar ballad 'Lavender's
Blue'. This was first written down in the late seven-
teenth century, and consisted of anything up to thirty
verses, many of them extremely bawdy and tiresomely
familiar, such as the young man insisting that the girl
he has his eye on loves his dog as well as him, and also
is obliged to love him in return for the illogical but
simple reason that he loves her. Down the centuries,
'Lavender's Blue' has been used or recorded by Ben-
jamin Britten, Vera Lynn, David Bowie and Disney's
2015 *Cinderella*, with Lily James. It is an example of a
song for everyone – a light-hearted song, admittedly,
but of universal appeal.

Something more serious but still on the same funda-
mental theme is Andrew Marvell's 'The Fair Singer':

> To make a final conquest of all me,
> Love did compose so sweet an enemy,
> In whom both beauties to my death agree,
> Joining themselves in fatal harmony,
> That, while she with her eyes my heart does bind,
> She with her voice might captivate my mind.

He is blown away, both by the singer and her voice
not a million miles, is it, from the frenzied adoration
surrounding modern pop idols, the fans who can hardly
separate – if indeed, they want to – the music from
the woman or the man. And poetry is the closest that
language comes to music, which can, after all, express
an intensity of human feeling that words sometimes
fail to reach. Poetry can also be a safe outlet, because
of its cultural acceptability, for a personal pain that is
too much to bear alone. And the fact that everyone on
the planet knows at some level what the poet is talking
about is balm to even the most tortured soul.

A. E. Housman certainly fell into the tortured cat
egory. In 1896, he published his famous *Shropshire
Lad*, which contained, among other poems, 'When I
was One-and-Twenty'. It is, deliberately I think, in
ballad style, in order to place it firmly in the category
of universal experience, but also to make the pain in
it more bearable because what he is describing is,
unique to Housman, far from unique in the realm of
human experience:

> When I was one-and-twenty
> I heard him say again,
> 'The heart out of the bosom
> Was never given in vain;
> 'Tis paid with sighs a plenty
> And sold for endless rue.'
> And I am two-and-twenty
> And oh, 'tis true, 'tis true.

So – love happens to everyone. Romantic or spirit
ual, sanctioned or forbidden, successful or frustrated
convenient or impossible, love is just there, for all of
us, like breathing. But so, in one way or another, is sex

And love poetry doesn't shrink from the sexual aspect of romantic love any more than it shrinks from pain. Here is Ben Jonson, in 1601, describing kissing:

> So sugared, so melting, so soft, so delicious,
>   The dew that lies on roses,
>   When the morn herself discloses,
>   Is not so precious. [. . .]
>   It should be my wishing
>   That I might die kissing.

Wilfred Owen takes rather a different view. Instead of rhapsodizing about how kissing makes him feel, he describes, almost bitterly, how sex has lured him down blind alleys, and then tossed him aside. There is no definite date to this poem – openly titled 'To Eros' – but it is known he revised it in 1917.

> In that I loved you, Love, I worshipped you,
> In that I worshipped well, I sacrificed
> All of most worth. I bound and burnt and slew
> Old peaceful lives; frail flowers; firm friends; and Christ.
>
> I slew all falser loves; I slew all true, [. . .]
>
> But when I fell upon your sandalled feet,
> You laughed; you loosed away my lips; you rose.
> I heard the singing of your wing's retreat;
> Far-flown, I watched you flush the Olympian snows
> Beyond my hoping. Starkly I returned
> To stare upon the ash of all I burned.

Sobering stuff, I know. But true, at least for some. Just as all the love poetry ever heard or written is true, for someone, somewhere, at some time. There is truth for each one of us, privately or for sharing, in a poem – or several – in this anthology.

POEMS FOR LOVE

WHAT IS LOVE?

What Is Love

Now what is love, I pray thee tell?
It is that fountain and that well
Where pleasure and repentance dwell.
It is perhaps that saucing bell
That tolls all into heaven or hell:
And this is love, as I hear tell.

Yet what is love, I pray thee say?
It is a work on holy day.
It is December matched with May,
When lusty bloods in fresh array
Hear ten months after of the play:
And this is love, as I hear say.

Yet what is love, I pray thee sain?
It is a sunshine mixed with rain.
It is a toothache, or like pain;
It is a game where none doth gain;
The lass saith No, and would full fain:
And this is love, as I hear sain.

Yet what is love, I pray thee show?
A thing that creeps, it cannot go;
A prize that passeth to and fro;
A thing for one, a thing for mo;
And he that proves must find it so
And this is love, sweet friend, I trow.

Sir Walter Raleigh (c.1554–1618)

Love What It Is

Love is a circle that doth restless move
In the same sweet eternity of love.

Robert Herrick (c.1591–1674)

To a Friend

I ask but one thing of you, only one.
That you will always be my dream of you;
That never shall I wake to find untrue
All this I have believed and rested on,
Forever vanished, like a vision gone
Out into the night. Alas, how few
There are who strike in us a chord we knew
Existed, but so seldom heard its tone
We tremble at the half-forgotten sound.
The world is full of rude awakenings
And heaven-born castles shattered to the ground,
Yet still our human longing vainly clings
To a belief in beauty through all wrongs.
O stay your hand, and leave my heart its songs!

Amy Lowell (1874–1925)

Love and Friendship

Love is like the wild rose briar,
Friendship, like the holly tree
The holly is dark when the rose briar blooms,
But which will bloom most constantly?

The wild rose briar is sweet in spring,
Its summer blossoms scent the air
Yet wait till winter comes again
And who will call the wild-briar fair?

Then scorn the silly rose-wreath now
And deck thee with the holly's sheen
That when December blights thy brow
He still may leave thy garland green –

Emily Brontë (1818–1848)

Love Will Find Out the Way

Over the mountains
And over the waves,
Under the fountains
And under the graves;
Under floods that are the deepest
Which Neptune obey,
Over rocks that are steepest,
Love will find out the way.

Where there is no place
For the glow-worm to lie,
Where there is no space
For receipt of a fly;
Where the midge dares not venture
Lest herself fast she lay,
But if Love come, he will enter
And will find out the way.

Some think to lose him
By having him confined;
And some do suppose him,
Poor heart! to be blind;
But if never so close you wall him,
Do the best that you may,
Blind Love, if so you call him,
Will find out his way.

You may train the eagle
To stoop to your fist;
Or you may inveigle
The phoenix of the east,

The lioness, you may move her
To give over her prey;
But you'll never stop a lover:
He will find out his way.

If the earth it should part him,
He would gallop it over;
If the seas should overthwart him,
He would swim to the shore;
Should his love become a swallow,
Through the air to stray,
Love will lend wings to follow,
And will find out the way.

There is no striving
To cross his intent;
There is no contriving
His plots to prevent;
But if once the message greet him
That his true love doth stay,
If death should come and meet him
Love will find out the way.

Anon.

Gifts

Give a man a horse he can ride,
 Give a man a boat he can sail;
And his rank and wealth, his strength and health,
 On sea nor shore shall fail.

Give a man a pipe he can smoke
 Give a man a book he can read:
And his home is bright with a calm delight,
 Though the room be poor indeed.

Give a man a girl he can love,
 As I, O my love, love thee;
And his heart is great with the pulse of fate,
 At home, on land, on sea.

James Thomson (1834–1882)

'Tune thy Music to thy heart'

Tune thy Music to thy heart,
Sing thy joy with thanks, and so thy sorrow:
  Though Devotion needs not Art,
Sometime of the poor the rich may borrow.

  Strive not yet for curious ways:
Concord pleaseth more, the less 'tis strained;
  Zeal affects not outward praise,
Only strives to shew a love unfained.

  Love can wondrous things effect,
Sweetest Sacrifice, all wrath appeasing;
  Love the highest doth respect,
Love alone to him is ever pleasing.

Thomas Campion (1567–1620)

Answer to a Child's Question

Do you ask what the birds say? The Sparrow, the
    Dove,
The Linnet and Thrush say, 'I love and I love!'
In the winter they're silent – the wind is so strong;
What it says, I don't know, but it sings a loud song.
But green leaves, and blossoms, and sunny warm
    weather,
And singing, and loving – all come back together.
But the lark is so brimful of gladness and love,
The green fields below him, the blue sky above,
That he sings, and he sings; and for ever sings he –
'I love my Love, and my Love loves me!'

Samuel Taylor Coleridge (1772–1834)

Love

It is to be all made of sighs and tears . . .
It is to be all made of faith and service . . .
It is to be all made of fantasy,
All adoration, duty and observance,
All humbleness, all patience, all impatience
All purity, all trial, all obedience . . .

William Shakespeare (1564–1616)

The Water Is Wide

The water is wide, I can't swim o'er
Nor do I have wings to fly
Give me a boat that can carry two
And both shall row, my love and I

A ship there is and she sails the sea
She's loaded deep as deep can be
But not so deep as the love I'm in
I know not if I sink or swim

I leaned my back against an oak
Thinking it was a trusty tree
But first it swayed and then it broke
So did my love prove false to me

Oh love is handsome and love is kind
Sweet as flower when first it is new
But love grows old and waxes cold
And fades away like the morning dew

Must I go bound while you go free
Must I love a man who doesn't love me
Must I be born with so little art
As to love a man who'll break my heart

Anon.

⤷ stop caring about
man that don't deserve it
and love and devote your
life to Jesus. He loves, cares
and is always there for you

13

from The Hunting of Cupid

What thing is love? for, well I wot, love is a thing.
It is a prick, it is a sting,
It is a pretty pretty thing;
It is a fire, it is a coal,
Whose flame creeps in at every hole;
And as my wit doth best devise,
Love's dwelling is in ladies' eyes:
From whence do glance love's piercing darts
That make such holes into our hearts;
And all the world herein accord
Love is a great and mighty lord,
And when he list to mount so high,
With Venus he in heaven doth lie,
And evermore hath been a god
Since Mars and she played even and odd.

George Peele (c.1556–1596)

If I Were Loved

If I were loved, as I desire to be,
What is there in the great sphere of the earth,
And range of evil between death and birth,
That I should fear, – if I were loved by thee?
All the inner, all the outer world of pain
Clear love would pierce and cleave, if thou wert mine,
As I have heard that, somewhere in the main,
Fresh-water springs come up through bitter brine.
Twere joy, not fear, clasped hand-in-hand with thee,
To wait for death – mute – careless of all ills,
Apart upon a mountain, though the surge
Of some new deluge from a thousand hills
Flung leagues of roaring foam into the gorge
Below us, as far on as eye could see.

Alfred, Lord Tennyson (1809–1892)

MADAM, WILL YOU WALK?

Madam, Will You Walk?

'I should like to buy thee a fine lace cap
With five yards of ribbon to hang down your back
If thou wilt walk with me.'

'I will not accept of the fine lace cap
With the five yards of ribbon to hang down my back
Nor I will not walk with thee.'

'I will buy thee a fine silken gown
With nine yards of ribbon to trail upon the ground
If thou wilt walk with me.'

'I will not accept of the fine silken gown
With nine yards of ribbon to trail upon the ground
Nor I won't walk with thee.'

'I'll buy thee a fine golden chair
To sit in the garden and to take the pleasant air
If thou wilt walk with me.'

'I will not accept of thy fine golden chair
To sit in the garden and to take the pleasant air
Nor I will not walk with thee.'

'It's I will give thee the keys of my chest
To take gold and silver when thou art distressed
If thou wilt walk with me.'

'I will not accept of the keys of your chest
To take gold and silver when I am distressed
Nor I will not walk with thee.'

'I'll give thee the key, O the key of my heart
And thy heart and my heart shall never depart
If thou wilt walk with me.'

'I will accept of the key of your heart
And thy heart and my heart shall never depart
And I will walk with thee.'

Anon.

Lavender's Blue

'Lavender's blue, dilly, dilly, lavender's green,
When I am king, dilly, dilly, you shall be queen.'
'Who told you so, dilly, dilly, who told you so?'
' 'Twas my own heart, dilly, dilly, that told me so.'

'Call up your men, dilly, dilly, set them to work
Some to the plough, dilly, dilly, some to the fork,
Some to make hay, dilly, dilly, some to cut corn,
While you and I, dilly, dilly, keep ourselves warm.'

'Lavender's green, dilly, dilly, lavender's blue,
If you love me, dilly, dilly, I will love you.
Let the birds sing, dilly, dilly, and the lambs play;
We shall be safe, dilly, dilly, out of harm's way.'

'If it should hap, dilly, dilly, if it should chance,
We shall be gay, dilly, dilly, we shall both dance.
Lavender's blue, dilly, dilly, lavender's green,
When you are king, dilly, dilly, I'll be your queen.'

Anon.

Tibbie Dunbar
(*Tune: Johnny Mcgill*)

O wilt thou go wi' me, sweet Tibbie Dunbar;
O wilt thou go wi' me, sweet Tibbie Dunbar;
Wilt thou ride on a horse, or be drawn in a car,
Or walk by my side, O sweet Tibbie Dunbar.

I care na thy daddie, his lands and his money,
I care na thy kin, sae high and sae lordly:
But say thou wilt hae me for better for waur,
And come in thy coatie, sweet Tibbie Dunbar.

Robert Burns (1759–1796)

Dining-Room Tea

When you were there, and you, and you,
Happiness crowned the night; I too,
Laughing and looking, one of all,
I watched the quivering lamplight fall
On plate and flowers and pouring tea
And cup and cloth; and they and we
Flung all the dancing moments by
With jest and glitter. Lip and eye
Flashed on the glory, shone and cried,
Improvident, unmemoried;
And fitfully and like a flame
The light of laughter went and came.
Proud in their careless transience moved
The changing faces that I loved.

Till suddenly, and otherwhence,
I looked upon your innocence.
For lifted clear and still and strange
From the dark woven flow of change
Under a vast and starless sky
I saw the immortal moment lie.
One instant I, an instant, knew
As God knows all. And it and you
I, above Time, oh, blind! could see
In witless immortality.
I saw the marble cup; the tea,
Hung on the air, an amber stream;
I saw the fire's unglittering gleam,
The painted flame, the frozen smoke.
No more the flooding lamplight broke
On flying eyes and lips and hair;

But lay, but slept unbroken there,
On stiller flesh, and body breathless,
And lips and laughter stayed and deathless,
And words on which no silence grew.
Light was more alive than you.
For suddenly, and otherwhence,
I looked on your magnificence.
I saw the stillness and the light,
And you, august, immortal, white,
Holy and strange; and every glint
Posture and jest and thought and tint
Freed from the mask of transiency,
Triumphant in eternity,
Immote, immortal.

               Dazed at length
Human eyes grew, mortal strength
Wearied; and Time began to creep.
Change closed about me like a sleep.
Light glinted on the eyes I loved.
The cup was filled. The bodies moved.
The drifting petal came to ground.
The laughter chimed its perfect round.
The broken syllable was ended.
And I, so certain and so friended,
How could I cloud, or how distress,
The heaven of your unconsciousness?
Or shake at Time's sufficient spell,
Stammering of lights unutterable,
The eternal holiness of you,
The timeless end, you never knew,
The peace that lay, the light that shone.
You never knew that I had gone
A million miles away, and stayed

A million years. The laughter played
Unbroken round me; and the jest
Flashed on. And we that knew the best
Down wonderful hours grew happier yet.
I sang at heart, and talked, and eat,
And lived from laugh to laugh, I too,
When you were there, and you, and you.

Rupert Brooke (1887–1915)

When I Was One-and-Twenty

When I was one-and-twenty
I heard a wise man say,
'Give crowns and pounds and guineas
But not your heart away;
Give pearls away and rubies
But keep your fancy free,'
But I was one-and-twenty,
No use to talk to me.

When I was one-and-twenty
I heard him say again,
'The heart out of the bosom
Was never given in vain;
'Tis paid with sighs a plenty
And sold for endless rue.'
And I am two-and-twenty
And oh, 'tis true, 'tis true.

A. E. Housman (1859–1936)

Afton Water

Flow gently, sweet Afton, among thy green braes,
Flow gently. I'll sing thee a song in thy praise;
My Mary's asleep by thy murmuring stream,
Flow gently, sweet Afton, disturb not her dream.

Thou stock dove whose echo resounds thro' the glen,
Ye wild whistling blackbirds in yon thorny den,
Thou green crested lapwing thy screaming forbear,
I charge you disturb not my slumbering Fair.

How lofty, sweet Afton, thy neighbouring hills,
Far mark'd with the courses of clear, winding rills;
There daily I wander as noon rises high,
My flocks and my Mary's sweet cot in my eye.

How pleasant thy banks and green vallies below,
Where wild in the woodlands the primroses blow;
There oft as mild ev'ning weeps over the lea,
The sweet scented birk shades my Mary and me.

Thy chrystal stream, Afton, how lovely it glides,
And winds by the cot where my Mary resides;
How wanton thy waters her snowy feet lave,
As gath'ring sweet flow'rets she stems thy clear wave.

Flow gently, sweet Afton, among thy green braes,
Flow gently, sweet river, the theme of my lays;
My Mary's asleep by thy murmuring stream,
Flow gently, sweet Afton, disturb not her dream.

Robert Burns (1759–1796)

A Red, Red Rose

My luve is like a red, red rose,
    That's newly sprung in June:
My luve is like the melodie,
    That's sweetly play'd in tune.
As fair art thou, my bonnie lass,
    So deep in luve am I,
And I will luve thee still, my dear,
    Till a' the seas gang dry.
Till a' the seas gang dry, my dear,
    And the rocks melt wi' the sun!
And I will luve thee still, my dear,
    While the sands o' life shall run.
And fare-thee-weel, my only luve,
    And fare-thee-weel a while!
And I will come again, my luve,
    Tho' it were ten thousand mile.

Robert Burns (1759–1796)

She Walks in Beauty

I

She walks in beauty, like the night
  Of cloudless climes and starry skies;
And all that's best of dark and bright
  Meet in her aspect and her eyes:
Thus mellow'd to that tender light
  Which heaven to gaudy day denies.

II

One shade the more, one ray the less,
  Had half impair'd the nameless grace
Which waves in every raven tress,
  Or softly lightens o'er her face;
Where thoughts serenely sweet express
  How pure, how dear their dwelling place.

III

And on that cheek, and o'er that brow,
  So soft, so calm, yet eloquent,
The smiles that win, the tints that glow,
  But tell of days in goodness spent,
A mind at peace with all below,
  A heart whose love is innocent!

George Gordon, Lord Byron (1788–1824)

To a Stranger

Passing stranger! you do not know
How longingly I look upon you,
You must be he I was seeking,
Or she I was seeking
(It comes to me as a dream)

I have somewhere surely
Lived a life of joy with you,
All is recall'd as we flit by each other,
Fluid, affectionate, chaste, matured,

You grew up with me,
Were a boy with me or a girl with me,
I ate with you and slept with you, your body has beco
Not yours only nor left my body mine only,

You give me the pleasure of your eyes,
Face, flesh as we pass,
You take of my beard, breast, hands,
In return,

I am not to speak to you, I am to think of you
When I sit alone or wake at night, alone
I am to wait, I do not doubt I am to meet you again
I am to see to it that I do not lose you.

Walt Whitman (1819–1

Thee, Thee, Only Thee

The dawning of morn, the daylight's sinking.
The night's long hours still find me thinking
    Of thee, thee, only thee.
When friends are met, and goblets crown'd,
  And smiles are near that once enchanted,
Unreach'd by all that sunshine round,
   My soul, like some dark spot, is haunted
    By thee, thee, only thee.

Whatever in fame's high path could waken
My spirit once, is now forsaken
    For thee, thee, only thee.
Like shores, by which some headlong bark
  To the ocean hurries, resting never,
Life's scenes go by me, bright or dark
   I know not, heed not, hastening ever
    To thee, thee, only thee.

I have not a joy but of thy bringing,
And pain itself seems sweet when springing
    From thee, thee, only thee.
Like spells that naught on earth can break,
  Till lips that know the charm have spoken,
This heart, howe'er the world may wake
   Its grief, its scorn, can but be broken
    By thee, thee, only thee.

           Thomas Moore (1779–1852)

Song

I hid my love when young while I
Couldn't bear the buzzing of a flye
I hid my love to my despite
Till I could not bear to look at light
I dare not gaze upon her face
But left her memory in each place
Where e'er I saw a wild flower lye
I kissed and bade my love goodbye

I met her in the greenest dells
Where dew-drops pearl the wood bluebells
The lost breeze kissed her bright blue eye
The bee kissed and went singing bye
A sunbeam found a passage there
A gold chain round her neck so fair
As secret as the wild bee's song
She lay there all the summer long

I hid my love in field and town
Till e'en the breeze would knock me down
The bees seemed singing ballads o'er
The flye's buzz turned a lion's roar
And even silence found a tongue
To haunt me all the summer long
The riddle nature could not prove
Was nothing else but secret love

John Clare (1793–1864)

First Love

I ne'er was struck before that hour
　With love so sudden and so sweet
Her face it bloomed like a sweet flower
　And stole my heart away complete
My face turned pale a deadly pale
　My legs refused to walk away
And when she looked what could I ail
　My life and all seemed turned to clay

And then my blood rushed to my face
　And took my eyesight quite away
The trees and bushes round the place
　Seemed midnight at noon day
I could not see a single thing
　Words from my eyes did start
They spoke as chords do from the string
　And blood burnt round my heart

Are flowers the winter's choice
　Is love's bed always snow
She seemed to hear my silent voice
　Not love's appeals to know
I never saw so sweet a face
　As that I stood before
My heart has left its dwelling place
　And can return no more –

John Clare (1793–1864)

Ruth

She stood breast high amid the corn,
Clasped by the golden light of morn,
Like the sweetheart of the sun,
Who many a glowing kiss had won.

On her cheek an autumn flush,
Deeply ripened; – such a blush
In the midst of brown was born,
Like red poppies grown with corn.

Round her eyes her tresses fell,
Which were blackest none could tell,
But long lashes veiled a light,
That had else been all too bright.

And her hat, with shady brim,
Made her tressy forehead dim; –
Thus she stood amid the stooks
Praising God with sweetest looks; –

Sure, I said, heaven did not mean,
Where I reap thou shouldst but glean,
Lay thy sheaf adown and come,
Share my harvest and my home.

Thomas Hood (1799–1845)

Meeting

Again I see my bliss at hand,
The town, the lake are here;
My Marguerite smiles upon the strand,
Unaltered with the year.

I know that graceful figure fair,
That cheek of languid hue;
I know that soft, enkerchiefed hair,
And those sweet eyes of blue.

Again I spring to make my choice;
Again in tones of ire
I hear a God's tremendous voice:
'Be counselled, and retire.'

Ye guiding Powers who join and part,
What would ye have with me?
Ah, warn some more ambitious heart,
And let the peaceful be!

Matthew Arnold (1822–1888)

The First Day

I wish I could remember the first day,
First hour, first moment of your meeting me,
If bright or dim the season, it might be
Summer or Winter for aught I can say.
So unrecorded did it slip away,
So blind was I to see and foresee,
So dull to mark the budding of my tree
That would not blossom yet for many a May.
If only I could recollect it, such
A day of days! I let it come and go
As traceless as a thaw of bygone snow;
It seemed to mean so little, meant so much;
If only now I could recall that touch,
First touch of hand in hand – Did one but know!

Christina Rossetti (1830–1894)

Episode of Hands

The unexpected interest made him flush
Suddenly he seemed to forget the pain, –
Consented, – and held out
One finger from the others.

The gash was bleeding, and a shaft of sun
That glittered in and out among the wheels,
Fell lightly, warmly, down into the wound.

And as the fingers of the factory owner's son,
That knew a grip for books and tennis
As well as one for iron and leather, –
As his taut, spare fingers wound the gauze
Around the thick bed of the wound,
His own hands seemed to him
Like wings of butterflies
Flickering in sunlight over summer fields.

The knots and notches, – many in the wide
Deep hand that lay in his, – seemed beautiful.
They were like the marks of wild ponies' play, –
Bunches of new green breaking a hard turf.

And factory sounds and factory thoughts
Were banished from him by that larger, quieter hand
That lay in his with the sun upon it.
And as the bandage knot was tightened
The two men smiled into each other's eyes.

Hart Crane (1899–1932)

The Look

Strephon kissed me in the spring
  Robin in the fall,
But Colin only looked at me
  And never kissed at all.

Strephon's kiss was lost in jest,
  Robin's lost in play,
But the kiss in Colin's eyes
  Haunts me night and day.

Sara Teasdale (1884–1933)

Love's Philosophy

The fountains mingle with the river
And the rivers with the ocean.
The winds of heaven mix for ever
With a sweet emotion;
Nothing in the world is single,
All things by a law divine
In one another's being mingle –
Why not I with thine?

See the mountains kiss high heaven
And the waves clasp one another;
No sister-flower would be forgiven
If it disdain'd its brother:

And the sunlight clasps the earth,
And the moonbeams kiss the sea –
What are all these kissings worth,
If thou kiss not me?

Percy Bysshe Shelley (1792–1822)

from Paradise Lost, Book IV

With thee conversing I forget all time,
All seasons and their change, all please alike.
Sweet is the breath of morn, her rising sweet,
With charm of earliest birds; pleasant the sun
When first on this delightful land he spreads
His orient beams, on herb, tree, fruit and flower,
Glistering with dew; fragrant the fertile earth
After soft showers; and sweet the coming on
Of grateful evening mild, then silent night
With this her solemn bird and this fair moon,
And these the gems of heaven, her starry train:
But neither breath of morn when she ascends
With charm of earliest birds, nor rising sun
On this delightful land, nor herb, fruit, flower,
Glistering with dew, nor fragrance after showers,
Nor grateful evening mild, nor silent night
With this her solemn bird, nor walk by moon,
Or glittering starlight without thee is sweet.

John Milton (1608–1674)

Down by the Salley Gardens

Down by the salley gardens my love and I did meet;
She passed the salley gardens with little snow-white
    feet.
She bid me take love easy, as the leaves grow on the
    tree;
But I, being young and foolish, with her would not
    agree.

In a field by the river my love and I did stand,
And on my leaning shoulder she laid her snow-white
    hand.
She bid me take life easy, as the grass grow on the
    weirs;
But I was young and foolish, and now am full of tears.

W. B. Yeats (1865–1939)

The Mower to the Glo-Worms

Ye living lamps, by whose dear light
The nightingale does sit so late,
And studying all the summer-night,
Her matchless songs does meditate;

Ye country comets, that portend
No war, nor prince's funeral,
Shining unto no higher end
Then to presage the grasses fall;

Ye glo-worms, whose officious flame
To wandering mowers shows the way,
That in the night have lost their aim,
And after foolish fires do stray;

Your courteous lights in vain you waste,
Since Juliana here is come,
For she my mind hath so displaced
That I shall never find my home.

Andrew Marvell (1621–1678)

The Glow-Worm

Among all lovely things my Love had been;
Had noted well the stars, all flowers that grew
About her home; but she had never seen
A glow-worm, never one, and this I knew.

While riding near her home one stormy night
A single glow-worm did I chance to espy;
I gave a fervent welcome to the sight,
And from my horse I leapt; great joy had I.

Upon a leaf the glow-worm did I lay,
To bear it with me through the stormy night:
And, as before, it shone without dismay;
Albeit putting forth a fainter light.

When to the dwelling of my Love I came,
I went into the orchard quietly;
And left the glow-worm, blessing it by name,
Laid safely by itself, beneath a tree.

The whole next day, I hoped, and hoped with fear;
At night the glow-worm shone beneath the tree;
I led my Lucy to the spot, 'Look here,'
Oh! joy it was for her, and joy for me!

William Wordsworth (1770–1850)

Scarborough Fair

Can you make me a cambric shirt,
  Parsley, sage, rosemary, and thyme,
Without any seam or needlework?
  And you shall be a true lover of mine.

Can you wash it in yonder well,
  Parsley, sage, rosemary, and thyme,
Where never sprung water, nor rain ever fell?
  And you shall be a true lover of mine.

Can you dry it on yonder thorn,
  Parsley, sage, rosemary, and thyme,
Which never bore blossom since Adam was born
  And you shall be a true lover of mine.

Now you've asked me questions three,
  Parsley, sage, rosemary and thyme,
I hope you'll answer as many for me,
  And you shall be a true lover of mine.

Can you find me an acre of land,
  Parsley, sage, rosemary, and thyme,
Between the salt water and the sea sand?
  And you shall be a true lover of mine.

Can you plough it with a ram's horn,
  Parsley, sage, rosemary, and thyme,
And sow it all over with one pepper-corn?
  And you shall be a true lover of mine.

Can you reap it with a sickle of leather,
  Parsley, sage, rosemary, and thyme,
And bind it up with a peacock's feather?
  And you shall be a true lover of mine.

When you have done and finished your work,
  Parsley, sage, rosemary, and thyme,
Then come to me for your cambric shirt,
  And you shall be a true lover of mine.

Anon.

First Sight of Her and After

A day is drawing to its fall
   I had not dreamed to see;
The first of many to enthrall
   My spirit, will it be?
Or is this eye the end of all
   Such new delight for me?

I journey home: the pattern grows
   Of moonshades on the way:
'Soon the first quarter, I suppose,'
   Sky-glancing travellers say;
I realize that it, for those,
   Has been a common day.

Thomas Hardy (1840–1928)

The Fair Singer

To make a final conquest of all me,
Love did compose so sweet an enemy,
In whom both beauties to my death agree,
Joining themselves in fatal harmony,
That, while she with her eyes my heart does bind,
She with her voice might captivate my mind.

I could have fled from one but singly fair;
My disentangled soul itself might save.
Breaking the curled trammels of her hair;
But how should I avoid to be her slave,
Whose subtle art invisibly can wreath
My fetters of the very air I breathe?

It had been easy fighting in some plain,
Where victory might hang in equal choice,
But all resistance against her is vain
Who has the advantage both of eyes and voice,
And all my forces needs must be undone
She having gained both the wind and sun.

Andrew Marvell (1621–1678)

A Thunderstorm in Town

(A Reminiscence: 1893)

She wore a new 'terra-cotta' dress,
And we stayed, because of the pelting storm,
Within the hansom's dry recess,
Though the horse had stopped; yea, motionless
    We sat on, snug and warm.

Then the downpour ceased, to my sharp sad pain,
And the glass that had screened our forms before
Flew up, and out she sprang to her door:
I should have kissed her if the rain
    Had lasted a minute more.

Thomas Hardy (1840–1928)

Farewell Nancy

farewell me dearest Nancy for now I must leave
  you,
ll across to the West Indies our course we must steer,
on't let me long voyage to sorry and grieve you
or you know I'll be back in the springtime of the
  year.

ne says, 'Like some little seaboy I'll dress and I'll go
  with you,
a the midst of all danger your help I'll remain;
a the cold stormy weather when the winds they are
  a-blowin',
 me love I'll be there to reef your top-sail.'

 your pretty little hands they can't manage our
  tackle,
our delicate feet in our clogs they'll cut so;
our little behind, love, would freeze in the wynde,
  love –
would have you at home when the stormy winds do
  blow.

o farewell me lovely Nancy for now I must leave you,
ll across the Western Ocean I am bound far away;
lthough we have parted, me love be true hearted
or you know I'll be back in the springtime of the
  year.

Anon.

IF ALL THE WORLD AND LOVE
WERE YOUNG

'If all the world and love were young'

If all the world and love were young,
And truth in every shepherd's tongue,
These pretty pleasures might me move
To live with thee and be thy love.

Time drives the flocks from field to fold,
When rivers rage and rocks grow cold,
And Philomel becometh dumb;
The rest complain of cares to come.

The flowers do fade, and wanton fields
To wayward winter reckoning yields;
A honey tongue, a heart of gall,
Is fancy's spring, but sorrow's fall,

Thy gowns, thy shoes, thy beds of roses,
Thy cap, thy kirtle, and thy posies
Soon break, soon wither, soon forgotten,
In folly ripe, in reason rotten.

Thy belt of straw and ivy buds,
Thy coral clasps and amber studs,
All these in me no means can move
To come to thee and be thy love.

But could youth last and love still breed,
Had joys no date nor age no need,
Then these delights my mind might move
To live with thee and be thy love.

Sir Walter Raleigh (c.1554–1618)

The Song of Wandering Aengus

I went out to the hazel wood,
Because a fire was in my head,
And cut and peeled a hazel wand,
And hooked a berry to a thread;
And when white moths were on the wing,
And moth-like stars were flickering out,
I dropped the berry in a stream
And caught a little silver trout.

When I had laid it on the floor
I went to blow the fire aflame,
But something rustled on the floor,
And some one called me by my name:
It had become a glimmering girl
With apple blossom in her hair
Who called me by my name and ran
And faded through the brightening air.

Though I am old with wandering
Through hollow lands and hilly lands,
I will find out where she has gone,
And kiss her lips and take her hands;
And walk among long dappled grass,
And pluck till time and times are done
The silver apples of the moon,
The golden apples of the sun.

W. B. Yeats (1865–1939)

Perspective

What seems to us for us is true.
    The planet has no proper light,
And yet, when Venus is in view,
    No primal star is half so bright.

Coventry Patmore (1823–1896)

Night Thoughts

Stars, you are unfortunate, I pity you,
Beautiful as you are, shining in your glory,
Who guide seafaring men through stress and peril
And have no recompense from gods or mortals,
Love you do not, nor do you know what love is.
Hours that are aeons urgently conducting
Your figures in a dance through the vast heaven,
What journey have you ended in this moment,
Since lingering in the arms of my beloved
I lost all memory of you and midnight.

Johann Wolfgang von Goethe (1749–1832)

Sudden Light

I have been here before,
    But when or how I cannot tell:
I know the grass beyond the door,
    The sweet keen smell,
The sighing sound, the lights around the shore.

You have been mine before, –
    How long ago I may not know
But just when at that swallow's soar
    Your neck turned so,
Some veil did fall, – I knew it all of yore.

Has this been thus before?
    And shall not thus time's eddying flight
Still with our lives our love restore
    In death's despite,
And day and night yield one delight once more?

Dante Gabriel Rossetti (1828–1882)

Balade Simple

O mighty goddess, day star after night,
Gladding the morrow when ye do appear,
To void darkness thorough freshness of your sight,
Only with twinkling of your pleasant cheer,
To you we thank, lovers that been here,
That this man – and never for to twin –
Fortuned have his lady for to win.

John Lydgate (c.1370–c.1451)

'Bright Star! would I were steadfast as thou art'

Bright Star! would I were steadfast as thou art –
Not in lone splendour hung aloft the night,
And watching, with eternal lids apart,
Like Nature's patient sleepless Eremite,
The moving waters at their priestlike task
Of pure ablution round earth's human shores,
Or gazing on the new soft-fallen mask
Of snow upon the mountains and the moors –
No – yet still steadfast, still unchangeable,
Pillowed upon my fair love's ripening breast
To feel for ever its soft fall and swell,
Awake for ever in a sweet unrest;
Still, still to hear her tender-taken breath,
And so live ever – or else swoon to death.

John Keats (1795–1821)

The Passionate Shepherd to His Love

Come live with me and be my Love,
And we will all the pleasures prove
That hills and valleys, dale and field,
And all the craggy mountains yield.

There will we sit upon the rocks
And see the shepherds feed their flocks,
By shallow rivers, to whose falls
Melodious birds sing madrigals.

There will I make thee beds of roses
And a thousand fragrant posies,
A cap of flowers, and a kirtle
Embroider'd all with leaves of myrtle.

A gown made of the finest wool,
Which from our pretty lambs we pull,
Fair linèd slippers for the cold,
With buckles of the purest gold.

A belt of straw and ivy buds
With coral clasps and amber studs:
And if these pleasures may thee move,
Come live with me and be my Love.

Thy silver dishes for thy meat
As precious as the gods do eat,
Shall on an ivory table be
Prepared each day for thee and me.

The shepherd swains shall dance and sing
For thy delight each May-morning:
If these delights thy mind may move,
Then live with me and be my Love.

Christopher Marlowe (c.1564–1593)

The Bait

Come live with me, and be my love,
And we will some new pleasures prove
Of golden sands, and crystal brooks,
With silken lines, and silver hooks.

There will the river whispering run
Warmed by thy eyes, more than the sun.
And there th' enamoured fish will stay,
Begging themselves they may betray.

When thou wilt swim in that live bath,
Each fish, which every channel hath,
Will amorously to thee swim,
Gladder to catch thee, than thou him.

If thou, to be so seen, be'st loth,
By sun, or moon, thou darkenest both,
And if myself have leave to see,
I need not their light, having thee.

Let others freeze with angling reeds,
And cut their legs, with shells and weeds,
Or treacherously poor fish beset,
With strangling snare, or windowy net:

Let coarse bold hands, from slimy nest
The bolded fish in banks out-wrest,
Or curious traitors, sleavesilk flies
Bewitch poor fishes' wandering eyes.

For thee, thou need'st no such deceit,
For thou thyself art thine own bait,
That fish, that is not catched thereby,
Alas, is wiser far than I.

John Donne (1573–1631)

Cherry-Ripe

There is a garden in her face
  Where roses and white lilies blow;
A heavenly paradise is that place,
  Wherein all pleasant fruits do flow:
    There cherries grow which none may buy
    Till 'Cherry-ripe' themselves do cry.

Those cherries fairly do enclose
  Of orient pearls a double row,
Which when her lovely laughter shows,
  They look like rose-buds filled with snow;
    Yet them nor peer nor prince can buy
    Till 'Cherry-ripe' themselves do cry.

Her eyes like angels watch them still;
  Her brows like bended bows do stand,
Threatening with piercing frowns to kill
  All that attempt with eye or hand
    Those sacred cherries to come nigh,
    Till 'Cherry-ripe' themselves do cry.

Thomas Campion (1567–1620)

An Hour with Thee

An hour with thee! When earliest day
Dapples with gold the eastern grey,
Oh, what can frame my mind to bear
The toil and turmoil, cark and care,
New griefs, which coming hours unfold,
And sad remembrance of the old?
     One hour with thee.

One hour with thee! When burning June
Waves his red flag at pitch of noon;
What shall repay the faithful swain,
His labour on the sultry plain;
And, more than cave or sheltering bough,
Cool feverish blood and throbbing brow?
     One hour with thee.

One hour with thee! When sun is set,
Oh, what can teach me to forget
The thankless labours of the day;
The hopes, the wishes, flung away;
The increasing wants, and lessening gains,
The master's pride, who scorns my pains?
     One hour with thee.

Sir Walter Scott (1771–1832)

Meeting at Night

I

The grey sea and the long black land;
And the yellow half-moon large and low;
And the startled little waves that leap
In fiery ringlets from their sleep,
As I gain the cove with pushing prow,
And quench its speed i' the slushy sand.

II

Then a mile of warm sea-scented beach;
Three fields to cross till a farm appears;
A tap at the pane, the quick sharp scratch
And blue spurt of a lighted match,
And a voice less loud, through its joys and fears,
Than the two hearts beating each to each!

Robert Browning (1812–1889)

I Will Make You Brooches

will make you brooches and toys for your delight
Of bird-song at morning and star-shine at night.
will make a palace fit for you and me,
Of green days in forests and blue days at sea.

will make my kitchen, and you shall keep your room,
Where white flows the river and bright blows the
broom,
And you shall wash your linen and keep your body
white
n rainfall at morning and dewfall at night.

And this shall be for music when no one else is near,
The fine song for singing, the rare song to hear!
That only I remember, that only you admire,
Of the broad road that stretches and the roadside fire.

Robert Louis Stevenson (1850–1894)

A Birthday

My heart is like a singing bird
  Whose nest is in a watered shoot;
My heart is like an apple tree
  Whose boughs are bent with thickset fruit;
My heart is like a rainbow shell
  That paddles in a halcyon sea;
My heart is gladder than all these
  Because my love is come to me.

Raise me a dais of silk and down;
  Hang it with vair and purple dyes;
Carve it in doves and pomegranates
  And peacocks with a hundred eyes;
Work it in gold and silver grapes,
  In leaves and silver fleurs-de-lys;
Because the birthday of my life
  Is come, my love is come to me.

Christina Rossetti (1830–1894)

Sonnet 18

Shall I compare thee to a summer's day?
Thou art more lovely and more temperate:
Rough winds do shake the darling buds of May,
And summer's lease hath all too short a date:
Sometime too hot the eye of heaven shines,
And often is his gold complexion dimm'd,
And every fair from fair sometime declines,
By chance or natures changing course untrimm'd:
But thy eternal summer shall not fade,
Nor lose possession of that fair thou owest,
Nor shall death brag thou wandrest in his shade,
When in eternal lines to time thou growest,
   So long as men can breathe or eyes can see
   So long lives this, and this gives life to thee.

William Shakespeare (1564–1616)

How Do I Love Thee?

I cannot woo thee as the lion his mate,
With proud parade and fierce prestige of presence;
Nor thy fleet fancy may I captivate
With pastoral attitudes in flowery pleasance;
Nor will I kneeling court thee with sedate
And comfortable plans of husbandhood;
Nor file before thee as a candidate . . .
I cannot woo thee as a lover would.

To wrest thy hand from rivals, iron-gloved,
Or cheat them by craft, I am not clever.
But I do love thee even as Shakespeare loved,
Most gently wild, and desperately for ever,
Full-hearted, grave, and manfully in vain,
With thought, high pain, and ever vaster pain.

Wilfred Owen (1893–1918)

He Wishes for the Cloths of Heaven

Had I the heavens' embroidered cloths,
Enwrought with golden and silver light,
The blue and the dim and the dark cloths
Of night and light and the half-light,
I would spread the cloths under your feet
But I, being poor, have only my dreams;
I have spread my dreams under your feet;
Tread softly because you tread on my dreams.

W. B. Yeats (1865–1939)

'Come into the Garden, Maud'

Come into the garden, Maud,
  For the black bat, night, has flown,
Come into the garden, Maud,
  I am here at the gate alone;
And the woodbine spices are wafted abroad,
  And the musk of the rose is blown.

For a breeze of morning moves,
  And the planet of Love is on high,
Beginning to faint in the light that she loves
  On a bed of daffodil sky,
To faint in the light of the sun she loves,
  To faint in his light, and to die.

All night have the roses heard
  The flute, violin, bassoon;
All night has the casement jessamine stirred
  To the dancers dancing in tune;
Till a silence fell with the waking bird,
  And a hush with the setting moon.

I said to the lily, 'There is but one
  With whom she has heart to be gay.
When will the dancers leave her alone?
  She is weary of dance and play.'
Now half to the setting moon are gone,
  And half to the rising day;
Low on the sand and loud on the stone
  The last wheel echoes away.

I said to the rose, 'The brief night goes
   In babble and revel and wine.
O young lord-lover, what sighs are those,
   For one that will never be thine?
But mine, but mine,' so I sware to the rose,
   'For ever and ever, mine.'

And the soul of the rose went into my blood,
   As the music clashed in the hall;
And long by the garden lake I stood,
   For I heard your rivulet fall
From the lake to the meadow and on to the wood,
   Our wood, that is dearer than all;

From the meadow your walks have left so sweet
   That whenever a March-wind sighs
He sets the jewel-print of your feet
   In violets blue as your eyes,
To the woody hollows in which we meet
   And the valleys of Paradise.

The slender acacia would not shake
   One long milk-bloom on the tree;
The white lake-blossom fell into the lake
   As the pimpernel dozed on the lea;
But the rose was awake all night for your sake,
   Knowing your promise to me;
The lilies and roses were all awake,
   They sighed for the dawn and thee.

Queen rose of the rosebud garden of girls,
   Come hither, the dances are done,
In gloss of satin and glimmer of pearls,
   Queen lily and rose in one;

Shine out, little head, sunning over with curls,
  To the flowers, and be their sun.

There has fallen a splendid tear
  From the passion-flower at the gate.
She is coming, my dove, my dear;
  She is coming, my life, my fate;
The red rose cries, 'She is near, she is near;'
  And the white rose weeps, 'She is late;'
The larkspur listens, 'I hear, I hear;'
  And the lily whispers, 'I wait.'

She is coming, my own, my sweet;
  Were it ever so airy a tread,
My heart would hear her and beat,
  Were it earth in an earthy bed;
My dust would hear her and beat,
  Had I lain for a century dead;
Would start and tremble under her feet,
  And blossom in purple and red.

Alfred, Lord Tennyson (1809–1892)

from Idem the Same,
A Valentine to Sherwood Anderson

Very fine is my valentine.
Very fine and very mine.
Very mine is my valentine very mine and very fine.
Very fine is my valentine and mine,
Very fine very mine and mine is my valentine.

Gertrude Stein (1874–1946)

DELIGHT IN DISORDER

Delight in Disorder

A sweet disorder in the dress
Kindles in clothes a wantonness.
A lawn about the shoulders thrown
Into a fine distraction;
An erring lace, which here and there
Enthralls the crimson stomacher;
A cuff neglectful, and thereby
Ribbons to flow confusedly;
A winning wave, deserving note,
In the tempestuous petticoat;
A careless shoestring, in whose tie
I see a wild civility;
Do more bewitch me than when art
Is too precise in every part.

Robert Herrick (c.1591–1674)

Sonnet

First time he kissed me, he but only kissed
The fingers of this hand wherewith I write,
And ever since, it grew more clean and white,
Slow to world-greetings, quick with its 'Oh, list,'
When the angels speak. A ring of amethyst
I could not wear here, plainer to my sight,
Than that first kiss. The second passed in height
The first, and sought the forehead, and half missed,
Half falling on the hair. O beyond meed!
That was the chrism of love, which love's own crown
With sanctifying sweetness, did precede.
The third upon my lips was folded down
In perfect purple state; since when, indeed,
I have been proud and said, 'My love, my own.'

Elizabeth Barrett Browning (1806–1861)

A Kiss

O, that joy so soon should waste!
   Or so sweet a bliss
     As a kiss,
Might not forever last!
So sugared, so melting, so soft, so delicious,
   The dew that lies on roses,
  When the morn herself discloses,
    Is not so precious.
O, rather than I would it smother,
Were I to taste such another;
   It should be my wishing
   That I might die kissing.

Ben Jonson (c.1572–1637)

The Shoe-Tying

Anthea bade me tie her shoe;
I did; and kissed the Instep too:
And would have kissed unto her knee,
Had not her Blush rebuked me.

Robert Herrick (c.1591–1674)

Sonnet 151

Love is too young to know what conscience is;
Yet who knows not, conscience is born of love?
Then, gentle cheater, urge not my amiss,
Lest guilty of my faults thy sweet self prove.
For thou betraying me, I do betray
My nobler part to my gross body's treason;
My soul doth tell my body that he may
Triumph in love; flesh stays no farther reason;
But, rising as thy name, doth point out thee
As his triumphant prize. Proud of this pride,
He is contented thy poor drudge to be,
To stand in thy affairs, fall by thy side,
    No want of conscience hold it that I call
    Her – love, for whose dear love I rise and fall.

William Shakespeare (1564–1616)

Wild Nights

Wild nights! Wild nights!
Were I with thee,
Wild nights should be
Our luxury!

Futile the winds
To a heart in port, –
Done with the compass,
Done with the chart.

Rowing in Eden!
Ah! the sea!
Might I but moor
To-night in thee!

Emily Dickinson (1830–1886)

Sonnet 57

Being your slave, what should I do but tend
Upon the hours and times of your desire?
I have no precious time at all to spend,
Nor services to do till you require.
Nor dare I chide the world-without-end hour
Whilst I, my sovereign, watch the clock for you,
Nor think the bitterness of absence sour
When you have bid your servant once adieu.
Nor dare I question with my jealous thought
Where you may be, or your affairs suppose,
But, like a sad slave, stay and think of naught
Save, where you are how happy you make those.
   So true a fool is love, that in your will,
   Though you do anything, he thinks no ill.

William Shakespeare (1564–1616)

My Sweetest Lesbia

My sweetest Lesbia, let us live and love;
And, though the sager sort our deeds reprove,
Let us not weigh them. Heaven's great lamps do dive
Into their west, and straight again revive.
But soon as once set is our little light,
Then must we sleep one ever-during night.

If all would lead their lives in love like me,
Then bloody swords and armour should not be;
No drum nor trumpet peaceful sleeps should move,
Unless alarm came from the camp of Love.
But fools do live and waste their little light,
And seek with pain their ever-during night.

When timely death my life and fortune ends,
Let not my hearse be vexed with mourning friends
But let all lovers, rich in triumph, come
And with sweet pastimes grace my happy tomb.
And, Lesbia, close up thou my little light,
And crown with love my ever-during night.

Thomas Campion (1567–1620)

Sonnet 130

My mistress' eyes are nothing like the sun;
Coral is far more red than her lips' red:
If snow be white, why then her breasts are dun;
If hairs be wires, black wires grow on her head.
I have seen roses damask'd, red and white,
But no such roses see I in her cheeks;
And in some perfumes is there more delight
Than in the breath that from my mistress reeks.
I love to hear her speak, – yet well I know
That music hath a far more pleasing sound;
I grant I never saw a goddess go, –
My mistress, when she walks, treads on the ground;
   And yet, by Heaven, I think my love as rare
   As any she belied with false compare.

William Shakespeare (1564–1616)

To His Coy Mistress

Had we but world enough, and time,
This coyness, Lady, were no crime.
We would sit down, and think which way
To walk, and pass our long love's day.
Thou by the Indian Ganges' side
Shouldst rubies find; I by the tide
Of Humber would complain. I would
Love you ten years before the flood:
And you should, if you please, refuse
Till the conversion of the Jews.
My vegetable love should grow
Vaster than empires, and more slow.
An hundred years should go to praise
Thine eyes, and on thy forehead gaze.
Two hundred to adore each breast:
But thirty thousand to the rest.
An age at least to every part,
And the last age should show your heart;
For, Lady, you deserve this state;
Nor would I love at lower rate.

But at my back I always hear
Time's wingèd chariot hurrying near:
And yonder all before us lie
Deserts of vast eternity.
Thy beauty shall no more be found;
Nor, in thy marble vault, shall sound
My echoing song: then worms shall try
That long-preserved virginity:
And your quaint honour turn to dust;
And into ashes all my lust.

The grave's a fine and private place,
But none, I think, do there embrace.
  Now, therefore, while the youthful glue
Sits on thy skin like morning dew,
And while thy willing soul transpires
At every pore with instant fires,
Now let us sport us while we may;
And now, like amorous birds of prey,
Rather at once our time devour,
Than languish in his slow-chapped power.
Let us roll all our strength, and all
Our sweetness, up into one ball:
And tear our pleasures with rough strife,
Thorough the iron grates of life.
Thus, though we cannot make our sun
Stand still, yet we will make him run.

Andrew Marvell (1621–1678)

Upon Julia's Clothes

When as in silks my Julia goes,
Then, then (me thinks) how sweetly flows
That liquefaction of her clothes.

Next, when I cast mine eyes and see
That brave Vibration each way free;
O how that glittering taketh me!

Robert Herrick (c.1591–1674)

My Woman

My woman says she wants no other lover
   than me, not even Jupiter himself.
She says so. What a woman says to an eager
   sweetheart
      write on the wind, write on the rushing
      waves.

Catullus (c.84–54 BC)

'Western wind, when wilt thou blow'

Western wind, when wilt thou blow
  The small rain down can rain?
Christ, if my love were in my arms
  And I in my bed again!

Anon.

'Your fair looks enflame my desire'

Your fair looks enflame my desire:
  Quench it again with love.
Stay, O strive not still to retire,
  Do not inhuman prove.
If love may persuade,
  Loves pleasures, dear, deny not;
Hear is a silent grovie shade:
  O tarry then, and flie not.

Have I seized my heavenly delight
  In this unhaunted grove?
Time shall now her fury require
  With the revenge of love.
Then come, sweetest, come,
  My lips with kisses gracing:
Here let us harbour all alone,
  Die, die in sweet embracing.

Will you now so timely depart,
  And not return again?
Your sight lends such life to my heart
  That to depart is pain.
Fear yields no delay,
  Secureness helpeth pleasure:
Then, till the time gives safer stay,
  O farewell, my lives treasure!

Thomas Campion (1567–1620)

To Celia

Drink to me only with thine eyes,
And I will pledge with mine;
Or leave a kiss but in the cup
And I'll not look for wine.
The thirst that from the soul doth rise
Doth ask a drink divine;
But might I of Jove's nectar sup,
I would not change for thine.

I sent thee late a rosy wreath,
Not so much honouring thee,
As giving it a hope that there
It could not wither'd be.
But thou thereon didst only breathe,
And sent'st it back to me;
Since when it grows, and smells, I swear,
Not of itself, but thee.

Ben Jonson (c.1572–1637)

The Canonization

or God's sake hold your tongue, and let me love,
    Or chide my palsy, or my gout,
y five grey hairs, or ruined fortune flout,
    With wealth your state, your mind with arts improve,
        Take you a course, get you a place,
        Observe his Honour, or his Grace,
    r the King's real, or his stamped face
    Contemplate; what you will, approve,
        So you will let me love.

las, alas, who's injured by my love?
    What merchant's ships have my sighs drowned?
ho says my tears have overflowed his ground?
    When did my colds a forward spring remove?
        When did the heats which my veins fill
        Add one more to the plaguy bill?
    oldiers find wars, and lawyers find out still
    Litigious men, which quarrels move,
        Though she and I do love.

all us what you will, we are made such by love;
    Call her one, me another fly,
e are tapers too, and at our own cost die,
    And we in us find the eagle and the dove,
        The phoenix riddle hath more wit
        By us; we two being one, are it.
    to one neutral thing both sexes fit
    We die and rise the same, and prove
        Mysterious by this love.

We can die by it, if not live by love,
    And if unfit for tombs and hearse
Our legend be, it will be fit for verse;
    And if no piece of chronicle we prove,
        We'll build in sonnets pretty rooms;
        As well a well wrought urn becomes
The greatest ashes, as half-acre tombs,
    And by these hymns, all shall approve
    Us canonized for love:

And thus invoke us; 'You whom reverend love
    Made one another's hermitage;
You, to whom love was peace, that now is rage;
    Who did the whole world's soul contract, and drov
        Into the glasses of your eyes
        (So made such mirrors, and such spies,
That they did all to you epitomize,)
    Countries, towns, courts: beg from above
    A pattern of your love!'

John Donne (1573–1631

'Blest, blest and happy he'

Blest, blest and happy he
Whose eyes behold her face,
But blessed more whose ears hath heard
The speeches framed with grace.

And he is half a god
That these thy lips may kiss,
Yet god all whole that may enjoy
Thy body as it is.

Anon.

Love and Sleep

Lying asleep between the strokes of night
   I saw my love lean over my sad bed,
   Pale as the duskiest lily's leaf or head,
Smooth-skinned and dark, with bare throat made
   to bite,
Too wan for blushing and too warm for white,
   But perfect-coloured without white or red.
   And her lips opened amorously, and said –
I wist not what, saving one word – Delight.
And all her face was honey to my mouth,
   And all her body pasture to mine eyes;
      The long lithe arms and hotter hands than fire
The quivering flanks, hair smelling of the south,
   The bright light feet, the splendid supple thighs
     And glittering eyelids of my soul's desire.

A. C. Swinburne (1837–1901)

The Sun Rising

Busy old fool, unruly sun,
   Why dost thou thus
Through windows and through curtains call on us?
Must to thy motions lovers' seasons run?
   Saucy pedantic wretch, go chide
   Late schoolboys and sour prentices;
Go tell court huntsmen that the king will ride;
   Call country ants to harvest offices:
Love, all alike, no season knows, nor clime,
Nor hours, days, months, which are the rags of time.

Thy beams, so reverend and strong
   Why shouldst: thou think?
I could eclipse and cloud them with a wink,
But that I would not lose her sight so long:
   If her eyes have not blinded thine,
   Look, and tomorrow late tell me
Whether both th' Indias of spice and mine
Be where thou leftist them, or lie here with me.
Ask for those kings whom thou sawst yesterday.
And thou shalt hear, all here in one bed lay.

She's all states, and all princes, I;
   Nothing else is.
Princes do but play us; compared to this,
All honour's mimic; all wealth alchemy.
   Thou, sun, art half as happy as we,
   In that the world's contracted thus;
Thine age asks ease, and since thy duties be
To warm the world, that's done in warming us.

Shine here to us, and thou art everywhere:
This bed thy centre is, these walls, thy sphere.

John Donne (1573–1631)

LET ME NOT TO THE MARRIAGE
OF TRUE MINDS

Sonnet 116

et me not to the marriage of true minds
dmit impediments. Love is not love
'hich alters when it alteration finds,
r bends with the remover to remove:
, no, it is an ever-fixed mark,
hat looks on tempests and is never shaken;
is the star to every wandering bark,
Vhose worth's unknown, although his height be taken.
ove's not Time's fool, though rosy lips and cheeks
'ithin his bending sickle's compass come;
ove alters not with his brief hours and weeks,
ut bears it out even to the edge of doom.
  If this be error and upon me proved,
  I never writ, nor no man ever loved.

William Shakespeare (1564–1616)

O Divine star of Heaven

O divine star of Heaven,
Thou in power above the seven;
Thou sweet kindler of desires
Till they grow to mutual fires;
Thou, O gentle Queen, that art
Curer of each wounded heart;
Thou the fuel, and the flame;
Thou in heaven, and here, the same;
Thou the wooer, and the wooed;
Thou the hunger; and the food;
Thou the prayer and the prayed;
Thou what is or shall be said.
Thou still young, and golden tressed,
Make me by thy answer blessed.

John Fletcher (1579–1625)

Sukey, you shall be my wife

Sukey, you shall be my wife
And I will tell you why:
I have got a little pig,
And you have got a sty;
I have got a dun cow,
And you can make good cheese.
Sukey, will you marry me?
Say Yes, if you please.

Anon.

Now

Out of your whole life give but a moment!
All of your life that has gone before,
All to come after it, – so you ignore
So you make perfect the present, – condense,
In a rapture of rage, for perfection's endowment,
Thought and feeling and soul and sense –
Merged in a moment which gives me at last
You around me for once, you beneath me, above me
Me – sure that despite of time future, time past, –
This tick of our life-time's one moment you love me!
How long such suspension may linger? Ah, Sweet –
The moment eternal – just that and no more –
When ecstasy's utmost we clutch at the core
While cheeks burn, arms open, eyes shut and lips me

Robert Browning (1812–18

from Monna Innominata:
A Sonnet of Sonnets

IV

I loved you first: but afterwards your love
Outsoaring mine, sang such a loftier song
As drowned the friendly cooings of my dove.
Which owes the other most? My love was long,
And yours one moment seemed to wax more strong;
I loved and guessed at you, you construed me
And loved me for what might or might not be –
Nay, weights and measures do us both a wrong.
For verily love knows not 'mine' or 'thine';
With separate 'I' and 'thou' free love has done,
For one is both and both are one in love:
Rich love knows naught of 'thine that is not mine';
Both have the strength and both the length thereof,
Both of us, of the love which makes us one.

Christina Rossetti (1830–1894)

Marriage Morning

Light, so low upon earth,
  You send a flash to the sun.
Here is the golden close of love,
  All my wooing is done.
Oh, the woods and the meadows,
  Woods where we hid from the wet,
Stiles where we stayed to be kind,
  Meadows in which we met!

Light, so low in the vale
  You flash and lighten afar;
For this is the golden morning of love,
  And you are his morning star.
Flash, I am coming, I come,
  By meadow and stile and wood,
Oh, lighten into my eyes and heart,
  Into my heart and my blood!

Heart, are you great enough
  For a love that never tires?
O heart, are you great enough for love?
  I have heard of thorns and briers.
Over the thorns and briers,
  Over the meadow and stiles,
Over the world to the end of it
  Flash for a million miles.

Alfred, Lord Tennyson (1809–1892)

I will give my love an apple

I will give my love an apple without e'er a core,
I will give my love a house without e'er a door,
I will give my love a palace wherein she may be,
And she may unlock it without any key.

My head is the apple without e'er a core,
My mind is the house without e'er a door,
My heart is the palace wherein she may be,
And she may unlock it without any key.

Anon.

from Love is Enough

Love is enough: though the World be a-waning,
And the woods have no voice but the voice of
   complaining,
   Though the sky be too dark for dim eyes to
   discover
The gold-cups and daisies fair blooming thereunder
Though the hills be held shadows, and the sea a dar
   wonder,
   And this day draw a veil over all deeds passed
   over,
Yet their hands shall not tremble, their feet shall not
   falter;
The void shall not weary, the fear shall not alter
   These lips and these eyes of the loved and the
   lover.

William Morris (1834–189

Oh wert thou in the cauld blast

Oh wert thou in the cauld blast,
   On yonder lea, on yonder lea;
My plaidie to the angry airt,
   I'd shelter thee, I'd shelter thee:
Or did misfortune's bitter storms
   Around thee blaw, around thee blaw,
Thy bield should be my bosom,
   To share it a', to share it a'.

Or were I in the wildest waste,
   Sae black and bare, sae black and bare,
The desert were a paradise,
   If thou wert there, if thou wert there.
Or were I monarch o' the globe,
   Wi' thee to reign, wi' thee to reign;
The brightest jewel in my crown,
   Wad be my queen, wad be my queen.

Robert Burns (1759–1796)

The Indian to His Love

The island dreams under the dawn
And great boughs drop tranquillity;
The peahens dance on a smooth lawn,
A parrot sways upon a tree,
Raging at his own image in the enamelled sea.

Here we will moor our lonely ship
And wander ever with woven hands,
Murmuring softly lip to lip,
Along the grass, along the sands,
Murmuring how far away are the unquiet lands:

How we alone of mortals are
Hid under quiet boughs apart,
While our love grows an Indian star,
A meteor of the burning heart,
One with the ode that gleams, the wings that gleam
    and dart,

The heavy boughs, the burnished dove
That moans and sighs a hundred days:
How when we die our shades will rove,
When eve has hushed the feathered ways,
With vapoury footsole by the water's drowsy blaze.

W. B. Yeats (1865–1939)

Song

Two doves upon the selfsame branch,
   Two lilies on a single stem,
Two butterflies upon one flower: –
   Oh happy they who look on them!

Who look upon them hand in hand
   Flushed in the rosy summer light;
Who look upon them hand in hand,
   And never give a thought to night.

Christina Rossetti (1830–1894)

from Song of the Open Road

Listen! I will be honest with you,
I do not offer the old smooth prizes, but offer rough
    new prizes,
These are the days that must happen to you:
You shall not heap up what is called riches,
You shall scatter with lavish hand all that you earn or
    achieve . . .

Allons! After the great Companions, and to belong to
    them!
They too are on the road – they are the swift and
    majestic men –
                    they are the greatest wom
Enjoyers of calm seas and storms of seas,
Sailors of many a ship, walkers of many a mile of land
Habitués of many distant countries, habitués of far-
    distant dwellings,
Trusters of men and women, observers of cities, solita
    toilers,
Pausers and contemplators of tufts, blossoms, shells o
    the shore,
Dancers at wedding-dances, kissers of brides, tender
    helpers of children,
                    bearers of children . . .

Camerado, I give you my hand!
I give you my love more precious than money,
I give you myself before preaching or law;
Will you give me yourself? will you come travel with m
Shall we stick by each other as long as we live?

Walt Whitman (1819–189

A Decade

hen you came, you were like red wine and honey,
nd the taste of you burnt my mouth with its sweetness.
ow you are like morning bread,
mooth and pleasant.
hardly taste you at all for I know your savour,
ut I am completely nourished.

Amy Lowell (1874–1925)

My Wife

Trusty, dusky, vivid, true,
With eyes of gold and bramble-dew,
Steel true and blade-straight,
The great artificer
Made my mate.

Honour, anger, valour, fire,
A love that life could never tire,
Death quench or evil stir;
The mighty master
Gave to her.

Teacher, tender, comrade, wife,
A fellow-farer true through life,
Heart-whole and soul-free,
The august father
Gave to me.

Robert Louis Stevenson (1850–1894)

The Owl and the Pussy-Cat

The Owl and the Pussy-Cat went to sea
 In a beautiful pea-green boat.
They took some honey, and plenty of money
 Wrapped up in a five-pound note.
The Owl looked up to the stars above,
 And sang to a small guitar,
'O lovely Pussy! O Pussy, my love,
What a beautiful Pussy you are,
    You are,
    You are!
What a beautiful Pussy you are!'

Pussy said to the Owl, 'You elegant fowl!
 How charmingly sweet you sing!
O let us be married! too long we have tarried:
 But what shall we do for a ring?'
They sailed away, for a year and a day,
 To the land where the Bong-Tree grows,
And there in a wood a Piggy-wig stood,
 With a ring at the end of his nose,
    His nose,
    His nose!
With a ring at the end of his nose.

'Dear Pig, are you willing to sell for one shilling
 Your ring?' Said the Piggy, 'I will.'
So they took it away, and were married next day
 By the turkey who lives on the hill.
They dined on mince, and slices of quince,
 Which they ate with a runcible spoon;

And hand in hand, on the edge of the sand
They danced by the light of the moon,
          The moon,
          The moon,
They danced by the light of the moon.

Edward Lear (1812–1888)

The Good-morrow

I wonder by my troth, what thou and I
Did, till we loved? were we not weaned till then?
But sucked on country pleasures, childishly?
Or snorted we in the seven sleepers' den?
'Twas so; but this, all pleasures fancies be.
If ever any beauty I did see,
Which I desired, and got, 'twas but a dream of thee.

And now good-morrow to our waking souls,
Which watch not one another out of fear;
For love all love of other sights controls,
And makes one little room an everywhere.
Let sea-discoverers to new worlds have gone,
Let maps to other, worlds on worlds have shown,
Let us possess one world, each hath one, and is one.

My face in thine eye, thine in mine appears,
And true plain hearts do in the faces rest;
Where can we find two better hemispheres
Without sharp North, without declining West?
What ever dies, was not mixed equally;
If our two loves be one, or thou and I
Love so alike that none do slacken, none can die.

John Donne (1573–1631)

Now You Will Feel No Rain

Now you will feel no rain,
for each of you will be a shelter to the other.

Now you will feel no cold,
for each of you will be warmth to the other.

Now there will be no loneliness,
for each of you will be a comfort to the other.

Now you are two persons,
but there is only one life before you.

Go now to your dwelling place,
to enter into the days of your togetherness.

And may your days be good
and long upon the earth.

Apache wedding song

The Anniversary

All kings, and all their favourites,
  All glory of honours, beauties, wits,
The sun itself, which makes times, as they pass,
Is elder by a year, now, than it was
When thou and I first one another saw:
All other things, to their destruction draw,
    Only our love hath no decay;
This, no tomorrow hath, nor yesterday,
Running it never runs from us away,
But truly keeps his first, last, everlasting day.

Two graves must hide thine and my corse,
  If one might, death were no divorce,
Alas, as well as other princes, we
(Who prince enough in one another be,)
Must leave at last in death, these eyes, and ears,
Oft fed with true oaths, and with sweet salt tears;
    But souls where nothing dwells but love
(All other thoughts being inmates) then shall prove
This, or a love increased there above,
When bodies to their graves, souls from their graves
  remove.

And then we shall be thoroughly blessed,
  But we no more, than all the rest.
Here upon earth, we are kings, and none but we
Can be such kings, nor of such subjects be;
Who is so safe as we? where none can do
Treason to us, except one of us two.
    True and false fears let us refrain,

Let us love nobly, and live, and add again
Years and years unto years, till we attain
To write threescore: this is the second of our reign.

John Donne (1573–1631)

'If thou must love me, let it be for nought'
(*Sonnets from the Portuguese, XIV*)

If thou must love me, let it be for nought
Except for love's sake only. Do not say
'I love her for her smile . . . her look . . . her way
Of speaking gently, . . . for a trick of thought
That falls in well with mine, and certes brought
A sense of pleasant ease on such a day' –
For these things in themselves, Beloved, may
Be changed, or change for thee, – and love, so wrought,
May be unwrought so. Neither love me for
Thine own dear pity's wiping my cheeks dry, –
Since one might well forget to weep who bore
Thy comfort long, and lose thy love thereby.
But love me for love's sake, that evermore
Thou may'st love on through love's eternity,

Elizabeth Barrett Browning (1806–1861)

To My Dear and Loving Husband

If ever two were one, then surely we.
If ever man were loved by wife, then thee.
If ever wife was happy in a man,
Compare with me, ye women, if you can.
I prize thy love more than whole mines of gold,
Or all the riches that the east doth hold.
My love is such that rivers cannot quench,
Nor ought but love from thee give recompence.
Thy love is such I can no way repay;
The heavens reward thee manifold, I pray.
Then while we live, in love let's so persever,
That when we live no more we may live ever.

Anne Bradstreet (1612–1672)

'How do I love thee?'
(Sonnets from the Portuguese, XLIII)

How do I love thee? Let me count the ways.
I love thee to the depth and breadth and height
My soul can reach, when feeling out of sight
For the ends of Being and ideal Grace.
I love thee to the level of everyday's
Most quiet need, by sun and candle-light.
I love thee freely, as men strive for Right:
I love thee purely, as they turn from Praise.
I love thee with the passion put to use
In my old griefs, and with my childhood's faith.
I love thee with a love I seemed to lose
With my lost saints! – I love thee with the breath,
Smiles, tears, of all my life! – and, if God choose,
I shall but love thee better after death.

Elizabeth Barrett Browning (1806–1861)

And You, Helen

And you, Helen, what should I give you?
So many things I would give you
Had I an infinite great store
Offered me and I stood before
To choose. I would give you youth,
All kinds of loveliness and truth,
A clear eye as good as mine,
Lands, waters, flowers, wine,
As many children as your heart
Might wish for, a far better art
Than mine can be, all you have lost
Upon the travelling waters tossed,
Or given to me. If I could choose
Freely in that great treasure-house
Anything from any shelf,
I would give you back yourself,
And power to discriminate
What you want and want it not too late,
Many fair days free from care
And heart to enjoy both foul and fair,
And myself, too, if I could find
Where it lay hidden and it proved kind.

Edward Thomas (1878–1917)

'Although I conquer all the earth'

Although I conquer all the earth,
Yet for me there is only one city.
In that city there is for me only one house;
And in that house, one room only;
And in that room, a bed.
And one woman sleeps there,
The shining joy and jewel of all my kingdom.

Anon.

The Bargain

My true love hath my heart, and I have his,
　By just exchange one for another given:
I hold his dear, and mine he cannot miss,
　There never was a better bargain driven:
　　My true love hath my heart, and I have his.

His heart in me keeps him and me in one,
　My heart in him his thoughts and senses guides:
He loves my heart, for once it was his own,
　I cherish his because in me it bides:
　　My true love hath my heart, and I have his.

Sir Philip Sidney (1554–1586)

Stella's Birth-Day

Stella this day is thirty-four,
(We shan't dispute a year or more:)
However, Stella, be not troubled,
Although thy size and years are doubled
Since first I saw thee at sixteen,
The brightest virgin on the green;
So little is thy form declined;
Made up so largely in thy mind.
O, would it please the gods to split
Thy beauty, size, and years, and wit!
No age could furnish out a pair
Of nymphs so graceful, wise, and fair;
With half the lustre of your eyes,
With half your wit, your years, and size.
And then, before it grew too late,
How should I beg of gentle fate,
(That either nymph might have her swain,)
To split my worship too in twain.

Jonathan Swift (1667–1745)

Fidelity

Fidelity and love are two different things, like a flower
    and a gem.
And love, like a flower, will fade, will change into
    something else
or it would not be flowery.

O flowers they fade because they are moving swiftly;
    a little torrent of life
leaps up to the summit of the stem, gleams, turns
    over round the bend
of the parabola of curved flight,
sinks, and is gone, like a comet curving into the
    invisible.

O flowers they are all the time travelling
like comets, and they come into our ken
for a day, for two days, and withdraw, slowly vanish
    again.

And we, we must take them on the wing, and let them
    go.
Embalmed flowers are not flowers, immortelles are
    not flowers;
flowers are just a motion, a swift motion, a coloured
    gesture;
that is their loveliness. And that is love.

But a gem is different. It lasts so much longer than
    we do
so much much much longer
that it seems to last forever.

et we know it is flowing away
s flowers are, and we are, only slower.
he wonderful slow flowing of the sapphire!

ll flows, and every flow is related to every other flow.
lowers and sapphires and us, diversely streaming.
n the old days, when sapphires were breathed upon
    and brought forth
uring the wild orgasms of chaos
ime was much slower, when the rocks came forth.
t took aeons to make a sapphire, aeons for it to pass
    away.

nd a flower it takes a summer.

nd man and woman are like the earth, that brings
    forth flowers
n summer, and love, but underneath is rock.
)lder than flowers, older than ferns, older than
    foraminiferae
lder than plasm altogether is the soul of a man
    underneath.

nd when, throughout all the wild orgasms of love
lowly a gem forms, in the ancient, once-more-molten
    rocks
f two human hearts, two ancient rocks, a man's heart
    and a woman's,
hat is the crystal of peace, the slow hard jewel of trust,
he sapphire of fidelity.
he gem of mutual peace emerging from the wild
    chaos of love.

D. H. Lawrence (1885–1930)

Love Song
(From the Gaelic)

My love, we will go, we will go, I and you,
And away in the woods we will scatter the dew;
And the Salmon behold, and the ousel too,
My love, we will hear, I and you, we will hear,
The calling afar of the doe and the deer.
And the bird in the branches will cry for us clear,
And the, cuckoo unseen in his festival mood;
And death, oh my fair one, will never come near
In the bosom afar of the fragrant wood.

W. B. Yeats (1865–1939)

MY LIFE CLOSED TWICE
BEFORE ITS CLOSE

'My life closed twice before its close'

My life closed twice before its close –
It yet remains to see
If Immortality unveil
A third event to me

So huge, so hopeless to conceive
As these that twice befell.
Parting is all we know of heaven,
And all we need of hell.

Emily Dickinson (1830–1886)

The Lost Love

She dwelt among the untrodden ways
   Beside the springs of Dove;
A Maid whom there were none to praise
   And very few to love:

A violet by a mossy stone
   Half-hidden from the eye!
– Fair as a star, when only one
   Is shining in the sky.

She lived unknown, and few could know
   When Lucy ceased to be;
But she is in her grave, and, oh,
   The difference to me!

William Wordsworth (1770–1850)

Remember

Remember me when I am gone away,
  Gone far away into the silent land;
  When you can no more hold me by the hand,
Nor I half turn to go yet turning stay.
Remember me when no more day by day
  You tell me of our future that you plann'd:
  Only remember me; you understand
It will be late to counsel then or pray.
Yet if you should forget me for a while
  And afterwards remember, do not grieve:
  For if the darkness and corruption leave
  A vestige of the thoughts that once I had,
Better by far you should forget and smile
  Than that you should remember and be sad.

Christina Rossetti (1830–1894)

Epitaph on the Monument of
Sir William Dyer at Colmworth, 1641

My dearest dust, could not thy hasty day
Afford thy drowsy patience leave to stay
One hour longer: so that we might either
Sit up, or gone to bed together?
But since thy finished labour hath possessed
Thy weary limbs with early rest,
Enjoy it sweetly: and thy widow bride
Shall soon repose her by thy slumbering side.
Whose business, now, is only to prepare
My nightly dress, and call to prayer:
Mine eyes wax heavy and the day grows old,
The dew falls thick, my blood grows cold.
Draw, draw the closed curtains: and make room:
My dear, my dearest dust; I come, I come.

Lady Catherine Dyer (c.1600–1654)

The Hill

Breathless, we flung us on the windy hill,
  Laughed in the sun, and kissed the lovely grass.
  You said, 'Through glory and ecstasy we pass;
Wind, sun, and earth remain, the birds sing still,
When we are old, are old . . .' 'And when we die
All's over that is ours; and life burns on
Through other lovers, other lips,' said I,
Heart of my heart, our heaven is now, is won!'

'We are Earth's best, that learnt her lesson here.
  Life is our cry. We have kept the faith!' we said;
  'We shall go down with unreluctant tread
Rose-crowned into the darkness!' . . . Proud we were,
And laughed, that had such brave true things to say.
— And then you suddenly cried, and turned away.

Rupert Brooke (1887–1915)

When You are Old

When you are old and grey and full of sleep,
And nodding by the fire, take down this book,
And slowly read, and dream of the soft look
Your eyes had once, and of their shadows deep;

How many loved your moments of glad grace,
And loved your beauty with love false or true,
But one man loved the pilgrim soul in you,
And loved the sorrows of your changing face;

And bending down beside the glowing bars,
Murmur, a little sadly, how Love fled
And paced upon the mountains overhead
And hid his face amid a crowd of stars.

W. B. Yeats (1865–1939)

A Church Romance

(*Mellstock, circa 1835*)

She turned in the high pew, until her sight
Swept the west gallery, and caught its row
Of music-men with viol, book, and bow
Against the sinking sad tower-window light.

She turned again; and in her pride's despite
One strenuous viol's inspirer seemed to throw
A message from his string to her below,
Which said: 'I claim thee as my own forthright!'

Thus their hearts' bond began, in due time signed.
And long years thence, when Age had scared Romance,
At some old attitude of his or glance
That gallery-scene would break upon her mind,
With him as minstrel, ardent, young, and trim,
Bowing 'New Sabbath' or 'Mount Ephraim'.

Thomas Hardy (1840–1928)

The Milking Hour

The sun had grown on lessening day
A table large and round
And in the distant vapours grey
Seemed leaning on the ground
When Mary like a lingering flower
Did tenderly agree
To stay beyond her milking hour
And talk awhile with me

We wandered till the distant town
Had silenced nearly dumb
And lessened on the quiet ear
Small as a beetle's hum
She turned her buckets upside-down
And made us each a seat
And there we talked the evening brown
Beneath the rustling wheat

And while she milked her breathing cows
I sat beside the streams
In musing o'er our evening joys
Like one in pleasant dreams
The bats and owls to meet the night
From hollow trees had gone
And e'en the flowers had shut for sleep
And still she lingered on

We mused in rapture side by side
Our wishes seemed as one
We talked of time's retreating tide
And sighed to find it gone

And we had sighed more deeply still
O'er all our pleasures past
If we had known what now we know
That we had met the last

John Clare (1793–1864)

I have lived and I have loved

I have lived and I have loved;
I have waked and I have slept;
I have sung and I have danced;
I have smiled and I have wept;
I have won and wasted treasure;
I have had my fill of pleasure;
And all these things were weariness.
And some of them were dreariness;
And all these things, but two things,
Were emptiness and pain:
And Love – it was the best of them;
And Sleep – worth all the rest of them,
Worth everything but Love to my spirit and my brain
But still my friend, O Slumber,
Till my days complete their number,
For Love shall never, never return to me again!

Charles Mackay (1814–1889)

Jenny Kiss'd Me

Jenny kiss'd me when we met,
    Jumping from the chair she sat in;
Time, you thief, who love to get
    Sweets into your list, put that in!
Say I'm weary, say I'm sad,
    Say that health and wealth have miss'd me,
Say I'm growing old, but add,
    Jenny kiss'd me.

Leigh Hunt (1784–1859)

Neutral Tones

We stood by a pond that winter day,
And the sun was white, as though chidden of God,
And a few leaves lay on the starving sod;
    – They had fallen from an ash, and were gray.

Your eyes on me were as eyes that rove
Over tedious riddles of years ago;
And some words played between us to and fro
    On which lost the more by our love.

The smile on your mouth was the deadest thing
Alive enough to have strength to die;
And a grin of bitterness swept thereby
    Like an ominous bird a-wing. . . .

Since then, keen lessons that love deceives,
And wrings with wrong, have shaped to me
Your face, and the God-curst sun, and a tree,
    And a pond edged with grayish leaves.

Thomas Hardy (1840–1928)

The Lost Mistress

All's over, then: does truth sound bitter
   As one at first believes?
Hark, 'tis the sparrows' good-night twitter
   About your cottage eaves!

And the leaf-buds on the vine are woolly,
   I noticed that, today;
One day more bursts them open fully
   – You know the red turns grey.

Tomorrow we meet the same then, dearest?
   May I take your hand in mine?
Mere friends are we, – well, friends the merest
   Keep much that I resign:

For each glance of the eye so bright and black.
   Though I keep with heart's endeavour, –
Your voice, when you wish the snowdrops back,
   Though it stay in my soul for ever! –

Yet I will but say what mere friends say,
   Or only a thought stronger;
I will hold your hand but as long as all may,
   Or so very little longer!

Robert Browning (1812–1889)

'April is in my mistress' face'

April is in my mistress' face,
And July in her eyes hath place,
Within her bosom is September,
But in her heart a cold December.

Anon.

To Eros

In that I loved you, Love, I worshipped you,
In that I worshipped well, I sacrificed
All of most worth. I bound and burnt and slew
Old peaceful lives; frail flowers; firm friends; and
  Christ.

I slew all falser loves; I slew all true,
That I might nothing love but your truth, Boy.
Fair fame I cast away as bridegrooms do
Their wedding garments in their haste of joy.

But when I fell upon your sandalled feet,
You laughed; you loosed away my lips; you rose.
I heard the singing of your wing's retreat;
Far-flown, I watched you flush the Olympian snows
Beyond my hoping. Starkly I returned
To stare upon the ash of all I burned.

Wilfred Owen (1893–1918)

'So, we'll go no more a roving'

I

So, we'll go no more a roving
So late into the night,
Though the heart be still as loving.
And the moon be still as bright

II

For the sword outwears its sheath,
And the soul wears out the breast,
And the heart must pause to breathe,
And love itself have rest

III

Though the night was made for loving,
And the day returns too soon,
Yet we'll go no more a roving
By the light of the moon.

George Gordon, Lord Byron (1788–1824)

'How many paltry, foolish, painted things'

How many paltry, foolish, painted things,
That now in coaches trouble every street,
Shall be forgotten, whom no poet sings,
Ere they be well wrapped in their winding sheet?
Where I to thee eternity shall give,
When nothing else remaineth of these dayes,
And Queens hereafter shall be glad to live
Upon the alms of thy superfluous praise;
Virgins and matrons reading these my rhymes,
Shall be so much delighted with thy story,
That they shall grieve, they lived not in these times,
To have seen thee, their sex's only glory:
    So shalt thou fly above the vulgar throng,
    Still to survive in my immortal song.

Michael Drayton (1563–1631)

I So Liked Spring

I so liked Spring last year
   Because you were here; –
     The thrushes too –
Because it was these you so liked to hear –
     I so liked you.

   This year's a different thing, –
    I'll not think of you.
But I'll like Spring because it is simply Spring
    As the thrushes do.

               Charlotte Mew (1869–1928)

The Stolen Heart

I prithee send me back my heart,
Since I cannot have thine;
For if from yours you will not part,
Why then shouldst thou have mine?

Yet now I think on't, let it lie,
To find it were in vain;
For thou hast a thief in either eye
Would steal it back again.

Why should two hearts in one breast lie,
And yet not lodge together?
Love! where is thy sympathy,
If thus our breasts thou sever?

But love is such a mystery,
I cannot find it out;
For when I think I'm best resolved,
I then am in most doubt.

Then farewell care, and farewell woe;
I will no longer pine;
For I'll believe I have her heart,
As much as she hath mine.

Sir John Suckling (1609–1641)

'Sigh no more, ladies, sigh no more'

Sigh no more, ladies, sigh no more.
　　Men were deceivers ever,
One foot in sea, and one on shore;
　　To one thing constant never.
　　　　Then sigh not so,
　　　　But let them go,
　　And be you blithe and bonny,
Converting all your sounds of woe
　　Into Hey nonny, nonny.

Sing no more ditties, sing no more,
　　Of dumps so dull and heavy!
　　The fraud of men was ever so,
　　Since summer first was leavy.
　　　　Then sigh not so,
　　　　But let them go,
　　And be you blithe and bonny,
Converting all your sounds of woe
　　Into Hey nonny, nonny.

William Shakespeare (1564–1616)

'An evil spirit your beauty haunts me still'

An evil spirit your beauty haunts me still,
Wherewith (alas) I have been long possessed,
Which ceaseth not to tempt me to each ill,
Nor gives me once, but one poor minute's rest:
In me it speaks, whether I sleep or wake,
And when by means, to drive it out I try,
With greater torments, then it me doth take,
And tortures me in most extremity;
Before my face, it lays down my despairs,
And hastes me on unto a sudden death;
Now tempting me, to drown my self in tears,
And then in sighing, to give up my breath;
    Thus am I still provoked, to every evil,
      By this good wicked spirit, sweet angel devil.

Michael Drayton (1563–1631)

How Can I Forget

That farewell voice of love is never heard again,
Yet I remember it and think on it with pain:
I see the place she spoke when passing by,
The flowers were blooming as her form drew nigh,
That voice is gone, with every pleasing tone –
Loved but one moment and the next alone.
'Farewell' the winds repeated, as she went
Walking in silence through the grassy bent;
The wild flowers – they ne'er looked so sweet before
Bowed in farewells to her they'll see no more.
In this same spot the wild flowers bloom the same
In scent and hue and shape, ay, even name.
  'Twas here she said farewell and no one yet
  Has so sweet spoken – How can I forget?

John Clare (1793–1864)

'Since there's no help, come let us kiss and part

nce there's no help, come let us kiss and part,
ay, I have done: you get no more of me,
nd I am glad, yea glad with all my heart,
hat thus so cleanly, I my self can free,
nake hands for ever, cancel all our vows,
nd when we meet at any time again,
e it not seen in either of our brows,
hat we one jot of former love retain;
ow at the last gasp, of love's latest breath,
hen his pulse failing, passion speechless lies,
hen faith is kneeling by his bed of death,
nd innocence is closing up his eyes,
    Now if thou wouldst, when all have given him over,
    From death to life, thou mightst him yet recover.

Michael Drayton (1563–1631)

Index of Poets

Index of First Lines

MACMILLAN COLLECTOR'S LIBRARY

Own the world's great works of literature in one beautiful collectible library

Designed and curated to appeal to book lovers everywhere, Macmillan Collector's Library editions are small enough to travel with you and striking enough to take pride of place on your bookshelf. These much-loved literary classics also make the perfect gift.

Beautifully produced with gilt edges, a ribbon marker, bespoke illustrated cover and real cloth binding, every Macmillan Collector's Library hardback adheres to the same high production values.

Discover something new or cherish your favourite stories with this elegant collection.

Macmillan Collector's Library: own, collect, and treasure

Discover the full range at
macmillancollectorslibrary.com